A New True Book

MUSIC

By Carol Greene

*This "true book" was prepared
under the direction of
Illa Podendorf,
formerly with the Laboratory School,
University of Chicago*

CHILDRENS PRESS, CHICAGO

Folk musicians

This book is for Debbie Carter, Dick Roberts, and the Emmanuel Junior Choir.

PHOTO CREDITS

James M. Mejuto—Cover, 2, 9 (bottom right), 11 (left), 32, 39

Historical Picture Service, Chicago—16, 36 (2 photos), 41 (2 photos)

Joseph A. DiChello, Jr.—9 (2 photos, top), 13, 30 (left), 34, 35 (left), 45 (right)

Tony Freeman—4, 9 (bottom left), 14, 21, 22 (2 photos), 24 (left), 26 (middle & right), 27 (bottom left and right), 28 (top & middle right), 33 (left), 35 (right)

Reinhard Brucker—11 (right)

Picture Group—©Alan Decker, 24 (right), 31; ©Ken Laffal, 26 (left); ©Lionel Delevingne, 28 (top left); ©Andrew Dickerman, 45 (left); ©Doug Bruce, 33 (right)

Tom Schiltz—25

Don & Pat Valenti—27 (top left)

Abbott Hunsucker—28 (bottom)

Hillstrom Stock Photos—©W.S. Nawrocki, 43; ©Milton & Joan Mann, 7, 30 (right)

Cover—Young people play in an orchestra

Library of Congress Cataloging in Publication Data

Greene, Carol.
  Music.

  (A New true book)
  Summary: Introduces the universal language of music, the families of musical instruments, and some of the great composers.
  Includes index.
  1. Music—Juvenile literature. [1. Music] I. Title.
ML3928.G73 1983   780   83-7255
ISBN 0-516-01701-2   AACR2

TABLE OF CONTENTS

School orchestra

THE LANGUAGE OF THE PLANETS

Wouldn't it be great if there were a language that everyone in the world could understand?

Well, in a way music is that language. Someone from Italy can write a piece of music. Someone from Australia can play it.

Someone from Norway can listen to it. And they all can understand what the music is saying.

That doesn't mean all music sounds alike. Chinese music sounds different from German music. Music written long ago sounds different from music written yesterday.

Mariachi band in Guadalajara, Mexico

But if you know the language of music—and listen long and hard—you can understand all kinds of music.

Thousands of years ago, some people believed that the planets made music. They thought the whole universe sang.

7

Today we send music into outer space. We send it with satellites. We send it in space capsules.

Now the universe really is singing. It is singing our music.

Maybe someday, creatures from another world will hear our music. Maybe they will listen long and hard. Maybe they will begin to

understand us because
of our music.
   Wouldn't that be great?

9

WHAT IS MUSIC?

Do you know what music is? You *know* when you hear it what music is. But it's hard to *tell* in words what music is.

Music is sounds and silences put together in a special way. (You'd better read that sentence again. It's tricky.)

Some people can play the piano without music. This is called "playing by ear." Others need to see the music in order to play.

You can't just close your eyes, pound on a piano, and call it music. You have to put the sounds and silences together on purpose.

A person who writes music is called a composer. Composers put the sounds and silences together. They write special symbols on special paper to show what the music should sound like.

This way of writing music is called notation. The paper with the music written on it is called a score.

Close-up of
a score

Another person can
pick up the score, read
the symbols, and play
the music. This person is
called a performer.

Bands often play for the crowds at football games.

But there must be at least one more person around to make the music really happen. That person is called—you guessed it!—the listener.

MUSICAL LANGUAGE

Music really *is* a language. You have to learn to understand it.

When you learn French or English, you study words, grammar, punctuation, and things like that. When you learn music, you study other things.

Melody is one important part of music. It is a group of sounds that come one after another. A melody is a little like a sentence in music.

Score showing the melody Ludwig van Beethoven wrote for a violin.

Some melodies are easy to hum. But some melodies are not easy to hum. Some are very short. Some are long.

Sometimes composers write a melody at the beginning of a piece of music. Then they take it apart and play with it for the rest of the piece. This is called development.

One musical note
played all by itself is just
one musical note. But if
you play two or more
different notes at the
same time, you have
harmony.

one note

harmony

These notes played
together are called a
chord.

Sometimes composers put chords under a melody. The chords make the melody stronger. It's a little like putting a foundation under a house.

Rhythm is how long or short the sounds and silences are. In a piece of music, this note ♩ is longer than this note ♪. This silence ▬ is longer than this silence 𝄾.

19

When you learn to read music, you learn how long to make each sound and silence.

Tempo is how fast or slow a piece of music is played. Sometimes music changes tempo. It may start fast, get slow, then get fast again.

   Changes in tempo can
change the way the
music makes us feel.
Sing a song you know
quickly. Then sing it
slowly. Tempo makes a
difference, doesn't it?

Flutes (left) and trombones (below) have different tone colors.

Tone color is the way
a musical note sounds
when an instrument plays
it. A note sounds one
way when a flute plays
it. It sounds different
when a trombone plays it.

It sounds still different
when a woman sings it.

Composers think a lot
about tone color when
they write music. They
try to give each note to
the instrument that will
make it sound the way
they want it to sound.
This is called orchestration.

MUSICAL INSTRUMENTS

Musical instruments come in families. There are six different families.

Harp (left) and cello (below)

This blue grass band plays country music with a banjo, two guitars, a mandolin, and a bass fiddle.

First is the strings family. The violin is in the strings family. So are the viola, cello, bass, harp, guitar, banjo, ukulele, and a few other instruments.

The clarinet (left), bassoon (middle), and saxophone (right) are in the woodwind family.

Once all woodwinds were made of wood. Now some are plastic or metal. The flute is in the woodwind family. So are the clarinet, oboe, bassoon, saxophone, and several other instruments.

The brass family is still
mostly made of brass.
Some of its members are
the trumpet, trombone,
French horn, and tuba.

The trumpet (left), French horn (below left), and tuba (below), are part of the brass family.

Percussion instruments
include the congas (below),
snare drums and cymbals
(top), and
kettledrums (right).
The organ (below) is
a keyboard instrument.

The percussion family has many different kinds of members. There are big kettledrums (timpani), snare drums, and bongos. There are gongs and cymbals, castanets and sleigh bells. There is even an instrument that sounds like horses' hooves.

The piano belongs to the keyboard family. So do the harpsichord, organ, and celesta.

An accordion (left) and bagpipes (right)

The sixth family
contains all the other
instruments. The
harmonica belongs to
this family. So do
bagpipes, accordions, and

electronic machines for making music.

Sometimes a performer can play a piece of music all alone. This is called a solo. Performers often play solos on the piano, organ, violin, or harp.

Close-up of a violin.

Brass quartet

Sometimes small groups of performers play music together. This is called chamber music. Often two violins, a viola, and a cello are played together. This called a string quartet.

String section of a symphony orchestra (left) and the famous conductor and composer, Leonard Bernstein (above)

When many different instruments play together, it is an orchestra. Usually a man or woman directs them so they play together correctly. This person is called a conductor.

Do you know what is
the oldest musical
instrument of all? It is
the human voice.

Composers write music
for women's or men's
voices, for high or low
voices. The highest
woman's voice is called

Left: Two performers are singing a duet.
Above: A large group of singers is called
a choir or chorus.

soprano. The lowest is
called alto. The highest
man's voice is called
tenor. The lowest is
called bass.

Singers can perform
alone or in small groups. A
large group of singers is
called a choir or a chorus.

THE STORY OF MUSIC

We know people made music thousands of years ago. They sang and played instruments in China and India, Egypt and Palestine, Greece and Rome.

Musical instruments were played in Egypt (left) and India (above) thousands of years ago.

These people painted pictures of themselves making music. But we don't know very much about how their music sounded. It was not written down.

The early Christians wrote music. It was sung by one person or a group of people in church. These songs or melodies were called plainsongs or chants.

Later, people began singing two or more melodies together. This was called polyphony. It was still sung mostly in church.

Finally composers began writing music to play outside of church. They wrote songs for voices and for instruments.

An Italian, Claudio Monteverdi, was the first important composer of operas. An opera is a story set to music and performed on a stage.

The opera *Aida* staged at the Royal Opera House in London, England.

By the 1700s people were writing music for instruments and voices. Two great composers were Johann Sebastian Bach and George Frederic Handel.

Wolfgang Amadeus Mozart and Franz Josef Haydn wrote many symphonies. A symphony is a long piece of music for orchestra.

Johann Sebastian Bach (left) and
Ludwig van Beethoven (above)
were famous composers.

Ludwig van Beethoven
wrote music that is full
of deep, powerful
feelings. Franz Schubert
wrote the same kind of
music. So did Felix
Mendelssohn, Robert
Schumann, Frederic
Chopin, and many others.

41

Today composers are experimenting with their music. Sometimes it is hard to understand. But we need to keep trying.

The kind of music Bach and Mozart wrote is called classical music. But there are other kinds of music, too.

A folk musician plays a "musical" saw.

People have sung, played, and danced to folk music for hundreds of years. No one knows who wrote it. People just learn it from one another. "Greensleeves" is a folk song.

Today many composers write popular songs. These songs are the ones we hear on the radio and television. Popular songs keep changing. But some of them stay popular for many years. "Jingle Bells" was once a popular song.

Jazz began with black people in the United States. Now people play

Saxophone player (left) and the Dixieland band (above) play different styles of jazz.

and sing it all over the world.

There are many kinds of music. You can enjoy all of them. Just learn the language, listen hard, and have fun!

WORDS YOU SHOULD KNOW

alto(AL • toh)—a low singing voice of a woman or boy or a man's high singing voice; lower than a soprano and higher than a tenor

bass(BAYSS)—the lowest man's singing voice

chamber music(CHAIM • ber)—music played by a small group of performers

chant—a song or melody with many words sung on the same note

chord(KORD)—a combination of three or more musical notes played at the same time

Christian(KRISS • chin)—someone who believes in Jesus Christ or follows a religion based on his teachings

classical music(CLASS • ih • kil)—music other than popular or folk music

composer(cum • POZE • er)—someone who writes music

conductor(Kun • DUCK • ter)—a person who leads an orchestra

foundation(foun • DAY • shun)—the lowest part of a structure

harmony(HAR • mun • ee)—one or more musical notes played with the melody

melody(MEL • oh • dee)—a group of musical notes played to produce a pleasing sound

notation(no • TAY • shun)—to write down music with symbols called notes

opera(OP • ra)—a musical play where the words are sung to music

orchestra(OR • kess • tra)—a group of musicians who play together on different instruments

orchestration(or • kess • STRAY • shun)—to decide what instrument will play each note so the music sounds best

percussion(per • KUSH • in)—a musical instrument in which sound is made by striking one thing against another

performer(per • FORM • er)—someone who entertains in some way

plainsong(PLAYN • song)—songs or chants sung at a church service

polyphony(puh • LIH • fun • ee) — to sing two or more melodies together

rhythm(RITHE • um) — a regular repeating of sounds

satellite(SAT • el • ite) — a man-made object that is put into space

score(SKOR) — the written form of music

solo(SO • loh) — a performance by one person

soprano(suh • PRAN • oh) — a high singing voice of a woman

space capsule(SPAYSS CAP • sul) — a type of aircraft that is sent into space

string quartet(STRING • kwor • TET) — a group of four musicians who play instruments that have strings

symbol(SIM • bil) — something that stands for something else

symphony(SIM • fon • ee) — a long piece of music written to be played by an orchestra

tempo(TEM • poh) — the speed at which music is played

tenor(TEN • er) — a man's singing voice higher than a baritone and lower than an alto

timpani(TIM • pan • ee) — kettledrums

tone color(TOAN • KUH • ler) — the sound of a note as it is played by different instruments

universe(YOO • nih • verse) — everything that exists, including the earth, planets, and space

INDEX

About the Author

Carol Greene has written over 25 books for children, plus stories, poems, songs, and filmstrips. She has also worked as a children's editor and a teacher of writing for children. She received a B.A. in English Literature from Park College, Parkville, Missouri, and an M.A. in Musicology from Indiana University. Ms. Greene lives in St. Louis, Missouri. When she isn't writing, she likes to read, travel, sing, do volunteer work at her church—and write some more. Her The Super Snoops and the Missing Sleepers *has also been published by Childrens Press.*